Discovering

FLOWERING PLANTS

Jennifer Coldrey

Artwork by Wendy Meadway

The Bookwright Press
New York · 1987

Discovering Nature

Discovering Ants
Discovering Bees and Wasps
Discovering Beetles
Discovering Birds of Prey
Discovering Butterflies and Moths
Discovering Crickets and Grasshoppers
Discovering Flies
Discovering Flowering Plants

Discovering Frogs and Toads
Discovering Rabbits and Hares
Discovering Rats and Mice
Discovering Snakes and Lizards
Discovering Spiders
Discovering Squirrels
Discovering Worms

Further titles are in preparation

All photographs from Oxford Scientific Films

First published in the
United States in 1987 by
The Bookwright Press
387 Park Avenue South
New York, NY 10016

First published in 1986 by
Wayland (Publishers) Limited
61 Western Road, Hove
East Sussex BN3 1JD, England

ISBN: 0–531–18098–0
Library of Congress Catalog Number: 86–62101

Typeset by DP Press Ltd., Sevenoaks, Kent
Printed in Italy by Sagdos S.p.A., Milan

Cover *This beautiful flower is a water lily.*

Frontispiece *A white-eye feeding on nectar from a bird of paradise flower.*

Contents

1
Introducing Flowering Plants

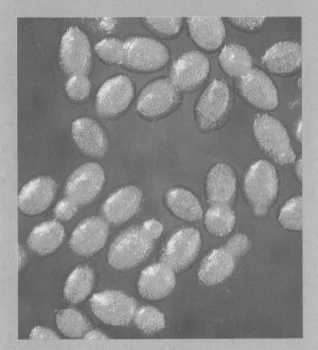

This rootless duckweed is the smallest flowering plant in the world.

Most of the plants we see around us are flowering plants. They are a large, successful group of plants and they grow in almost every kind of place you can think of. They include grasses, shrubs and many trees, as well as familiar flowers like daisies and roses. They do not include ferns, mosses, lichens, and the cone-bearing trees, none of which form true flowers.

There are well over a quarter of a million different kinds of flowering plants in the world, and most of these are tropical. The tallest flowering plants are the Australian gum trees some of which reach 150 meters (500 ft) in height. By contrast, the smallest flowering plant is hardly bigger than a pinhead. It is a tiny, green duckweed, a leaf-like blob, which floats on the surface of ponds and lakes in warm countries.

Some plants are specially suited to living in woodland, others will only grow in grassland or moorland, in bogs or marshes, or by the ocean. Many plants live in tropical jungles where it is moist and warm all year round. Others live on cold, high mountains, while some can survive in the desert. Every **habitat** has its own particular kind of soil and climate and these affect the plants that are able to grow there. Even in our own gardens, we can only grow certain flowers by changing the soil or other conditions.

The largest flower in the world is called Rafflesia. The huge, pink flowers measure 1 meter (3 ft) across.

2
What is a Flowering Plant?

Carrots, like many of the root vegetables we eat, are tap roots. These carrots have been damaged by the grubs of the carrot root fly.

Starting at the Roots

Flowering plants come in many different shapes, sizes and colors, but they all have the same basic design. They all consist of roots, stems, leaves and flowers, and nearly all of them produce seeds.

The roots of most flowering plants grow down into the soil and help to anchor the plant firmly in the ground. The roots also take in water, which contains important **minerals**. These pass up inside the plant to the parts above ground. Plant roots are covered with many tiny hairs and it is these that absorb the water from the soil.

Some plants have a cluster of thin, spreading roots, all of roughly the same length and thickness. These are called fibrous roots. Other plants have one thick, main root with smaller roots sprouting from it. The thick root is called the tap root. If you dig up a dandelion you will see it has a central tap root, unlike a buttercup which has a mass of fibrous roots. Tap roots are often fat and swollen – they store food for the plant, so that it can survive during winter when the parts above ground die off. Many of the vegetables we eat, such as carrots and turnips, are the swollen tap roots of flowering plants.

Some plants have shallow roots, which only spread through the upper layers of the soil. Other plants have long, deep roots. Trees and other tall plants have very big roots, which hold them steady in the ground. Some trees have roots that reach as deep as 18 meters (58 ft) underground. Trees absorb enormous amounts of water through their roots, some as much as 340 liters (75 gal) every day.

Trees have large roots to hold them firmly in the ground. The soil around the base of this beech tree has been worn away, exposing the tree's roots.

Shoots and Stems

The shoot or stem of a flowering plant normally grows above the ground and bears the leaves and flowers. It may have many branches. The shoot connects the roots to the other parts of the plant. It is the main transportation system and contains long, tube-like cells, which carry food and water to different parts of the plant. Water and salts are carried up from the roots, while sugars are carried down from the leaves.

Most plants have strong, upright stems, which support the flowers and hold the leaves toward the light. Some plant stems are rounded and smooth on the surface, some are ridged or rough in texture, while others

Trees have strong, woody stems. Their trunks and branches are covered with a thick layer of bark.

are covered with hairs or prickles.

Some flowering plants have thin, weak stems that can only support themselves by creeping or clinging to other things. The stems of the wild strawberry creep along the ground. Vetches cling to other plants with finger-like tendrils, while creepers like ivy clutch at walls or tree trunks with special small roots or suckers. Some plants use hooks or thorns to help them cling.

Several flowering plants have underground stems, which they use to store food. A potato is, in fact, the swollen tip of an underground stem. The crocus stores food in its **corm**, the fat, round part of the stem just below the ground, while iris and ginger plants have swollen underground stems called **rhizomes**.

Bindweed climbs by winding its stem around other plants.

Leaves for Making Food

The leaves of a flowering plant are very important because they are the "factories" that make the food for the rest of the plant. The process by which leaves make food is called **photosynthesis**. Leaves contain a green substance called **chlorophyll**, which can absorb the energy from sunlight and so help to change simple chemicals (carbon dioxide and water) into sugars. Carbon dioxide is a gas that the leaves take in from the air through small holes on their surface, called **stomata**. Oxygen for breathing is also taken in through these holes. Any waste gases pass out through the stomata. Plants lose a lot of water through their leaves too, but in dry weather the stomata usually close up to conserve moisture.

The food made in the leaves is carried to the stems along special channels called **veins**. The stems then carry the food away to other parts of the plant. The veins also carry water and minerals, which come in through the stem, to all parts of the leaf.

The leaves of flowering plants have many different shapes and forms. They can be long, thin and tapering, broad, oval, heart-shaped or circular. Some have wavy or jagged edges, others have smooth edges; some are

You can clearly see the network of food-carrying veins in this oak leaf.

Onion plants store food at the base of the leaf in the form of a bulb.

Some flowering plants, like this yellow iris, have the veins arranged in long, parallel lines down their leaves.

thin and papery, others tough and leathery; some are rough and hairy, others smooth and shiny.

Flowering plants such as the daffodil, tulip, onion and hyacinth, store food at the base of their leaves to help them survive from year to year. The overlapping leaves swell up at the bottom to form the bulging, underground food store that we call a **bulb**.

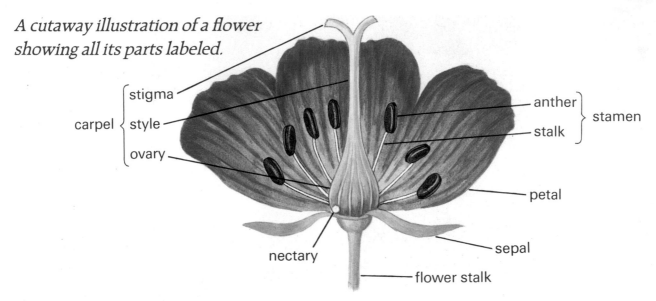

A cutaway illustration of a flower showing all its parts labeled.

Flowers for Reproduction

The flowers are important in the life cycle of a plant because they contain the male and female parts that are needed for **reproduction**.

Outside the large and usually colorful petals is a ring of green, leaf-like structures called **sepals**. These protect the flower when it is in bud.

The female parts are at the center of the flower. Each unit, called a **carpel**, has an **ovary** at the base, which contains one or more tiny egg cells or **ovules**. A buttercup has several carpels, but some flowers have only one carpel in each flower. Sticking up from each ovary is a stalk called a **style**. The tip of the style, which is often sticky, is called the **stigma**.

The male parts, or **stamens**, of most flowers are arranged outside the female parts. Each stamen has a stalk bearing a swollen head called the

Cowslip flowers hang down in clusters.

anther. When ripe, the anthers burst open to produce clouds of dusty **pollen**.

There are hundreds of different shapes, colors and designs of flowers. Many are open and cup-shaped, while others have the petals joined to form a trumpet-like tube, with the sexual parts hidden deep inside the flower. Some plants have only one flower on each stem, while others have a cluster, or tall spike, of flowers on one stem.

The flowers of some plants are small and dull with no petals at all, but most flowers are brightly colored and often sweetly scented, which attracts insects. Many produce nectar, a sweet, sugary liquid, which is found in pouch-like **nectaries** at the base of the petals.

The flowers of ox-eye daisies are arranged into flat disks.

3
How Flowering Plants Reproduce

The hazel tree has separate male and female flowers. The long, pale green male flowers are called catkins.

What is Pollination?

Flowers are produced at a very important stage in the life cycle of a plant. Their job is to form fruits and seeds from which new plants will grow. But before they can make seeds, flowers have to be **fertilized** and this can only happen if pollen grains are carried to the stigma of a similar type of flower. This process is called **pollination**.

When a pollen grain lands on the stigma, it puts out a tube that grows down inside the style until it reaches an ovule inside the ovary. The ovule becomes fertilized when the contents of the pollen tube join with it. It is now able to grow into a seed.

Although many flowering plants can be fertilized by their own pollen, most plants produce stronger, healthier offspring if they are fertilized by pollen from another plant

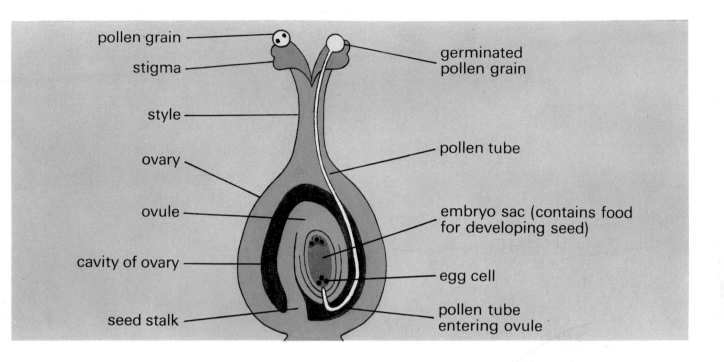

pollen grain

stigma

style

ovary

ovule

cavity of ovary

seed stalk

germinated
pollen grain

pollen tube

embryo sac (contains food
for developing seed)

egg cell

pollen tube
entering ovule

of the same kind.

Many flowers have male and female parts close together in the same flower, but they avoid pollinating themselves in various ways. The stamens and stigma of many flowers ripen at different times so that when the stamens are shedding their pollen, the stigma is not ready to receive it.

A cutaway illustration of a carpel showing how a flower is fertilized by pollen.

Some plants, like the hazel tree, avoid self-pollination by having their stamens and stigmas in separate flowers on the same plant. Others, including many trees, have totally separate male and female plants.

Pollination by Insects

Most brightly colored flowers are pollinated by insects. Bees, butterflies, wasps, flies and beetles all visit flowers to feed on nectar or pollen. They are attracted to the flowers by their color and scent, and, as they crawl among the petals, they brush against the stamens and pick up pollen which sticks to their bodies. Some of this pollen may then get

In this dandelion flower, the pollen and nectar are easy to find so it is visited by many insects, including flower flies.

rubbed off on to the next flower they visit. If it lands on the stigma of a similar type of flower, the flower will be pollinated.

Flowers have developed various shapes and designs that attract insects. The petals of many flowers form a flat or saucer-shaped disk, which provides a useful landing platform for insects. Some orchids are so highly specialized that there is only one particular kind of bee that can get inside the flower and pollinate it.

Some flowers have petals streaked with spots or lines of color, which lead insects toward the center of the flower where the nectar lies. These lines are called "honey-guides." Flowers pollinated by moths give out most of their scent at night. They are often white or pale in colour, which shows up well in the dark and attracts the night-flying moths.

Not all flowers smell sweet – some,

An elephant hawk moth visiting honeysuckle. Some flowers have their nectar hidden at the bottom of long, joined, tube-like petals. Only insects with long tongues, such as butterflies and moths, can reach the nectar and pollinate the flowers.

including the wild arums and the giant *Rafflesia*, smell of rotten flesh or dung. This attracts flies, which pollinate them.

Other Methods of Pollination

In many parts of the world, especially tropical countries, birds, and sometimes even mammals, pollinate the flowers. In North and South America, hummingbirds feed on nectar, carrying pollen on their bodies as they fly from flower to flower. In South Africa and Australia, many flowers are pollinated by small mammals, including rats, mice and small possums. Nectar and pollen-feeding bats are common in many tropical countries; like moths, they are night-time visitors, but are often attracted to flowers with stale, unpleasant smells.

Some flowers use the wind to

In Australia, a little animal called the honey possum pollinates the flowers of the coral gum tree as it sips the sweet nectar from around the bottom of the stamens.

spread their pollen from flower to flower. Grasses, sedges, nettles, plantains and the flowers of many trees are pollinated by the wind. These plants have no need of big, colorful flowers; instead, their flowers are small and pale, often without petals, and rarely have any scent or nectar. Their stamens have very long stalks, which hang out of the flower when ripe, so that they can be easily shaken by the wind. Their stigmas also poke out of the flowers. They are long, feathery and often sticky, which helps to trap any pollen grains that float by in the wind.

Being so light, the pollen grains are carried long distances through the air. A lot of pollen is wasted when it is blown away by the wind. Wind-pollinated flowers produce enormous amounts of pollen, so some pollen grains, at least, will land on female flowers and fertilize them.

Rye grass flowers shedding pollen, which is carried to other plants by the wind.

Making Fruits and Seeds

Once the ovules of a flower have been fertilized, they start to grow and change into seeds. The ovary around them also grows and slowly changes into a fruit that will protect and cover the seeds. Eventually the petals, sepals and stamens wither and die. They are not needed any more.

Some fruits, such as plums and blackberries, become soft, sweet and juicy. Other plants, such as the poppy

The seeds of the marsh marigold form inside pod-like clusters.

and snapdragon, have dry, flask-like seed-boxes, while members of the pea family produce their seeds in a pod. The fruit of the oak tree is an acorn. Many other trees produce hard-shelled fruits called nuts. Some fruits have only one seed inside them, for example plums and cherries, while other fruits, like apples and tomatoes, contain many seeds.

Plants spread their seeds in various ways. Juicy fruits and berries are usually eaten by birds and other animals. The seeds pass through the animal's body and come out in the droppings, usually far away from the parent plant. Many pod-like fruits explode when they are ripe, and the seeds are scattered. Many seeds are spread by the wind.

The seeds of some water plants have a spongy covering, or an air-filled coat, so that they can float away before they sink and start to grow.

Some fruits are covered with tiny hooks, which cling to animals' fur and so get carried away.

Thistle seeds float away in the wind using their fluffy parasols of hairs as parachutes.

The Growth of New Plants

Inside every seed there is an **embryo** plant. This consists of a tiny root, a tiny shoot and either one or two large, swollen seed-leaves or **cotyledons**.

The embryo plant will start to grow only when the conditions are just right. First the seed must land, or be planted, on the right kind of soil. It then needs to have the right amount of warmth, air and moisture before it will **germinate**. Some seeds, such as cress, germinate very quickly after they are planted; others may lie in the ground for several years before the seed coat rots away and allows the young plant to grow.

At the start of germination, a seed absorbs water and begins to swell. Eventually, the seed coat splits and the young seedling starts to appear. A tiny root grows down into the soil, while the shoot grows up toward the

Above left *A broad bean seed starts to germinate. The cotyledons, which stay below the ground, contain a store of food for the young plant.* Above right *Once above ground the shoot turns green and produces its first, true leaves. The seedling is now well on the way to becoming the same kind of plant as its parents.*

light. In some plants, the cotyledons stay below ground, while in others, they are carried above ground where they act like true leaves. However, the cotyledons eventually shrivel and disappear as their food supplies are used up by the plant.

New plants do not always grow from seeds. Some flowering plants produce baby plants from buds on their stems or leaves. These youngsters eventually break off from the parent to become separate new plants. Plants with bulbs, such as daffodils and hyacinths, produce new plants that form as buds on the parent bulb.

Strawberry plants send out long creeping stems, or runners, which produce new plants at various points where they touch the ground and take root.

A field full of red poppies and corn marigolds. These two annuals grow from seed, flower, set seed and die, all in one season.

Life Cycles

Flowering plants live for different lengths of time. Plants that live for one year or less are called **annuals**. In order to produce a new crop of flowers, their seeds must survive until the next growing season.

Plants that live for only two years are called **biennials**. In the first year they grow from seed, developing leaves that produce food for the plant to store over winter. During the winter the plants stop growing. They stay alive, but rest until spring returns, when they use their stored food to grow and flower. The flowers make seeds and then the plant dies.

Perennials are flowering plants that can live for many years. They include trees and shrubs, as well as many non-woody plants. Like biennials, perennials survive bad weather by resting and storing food,

ready for growth when the good weather returns. Plants with underground bulbs, corms, tubers or rhizomes are all perennials, which store food in times of hardship. Perennials also flower and form seeds, but they do not have to rely on their seeds for survival every year.

In tropical countries it is warm all year round. Providing it is moist,

Bluebells are perennial plants that survive from year to year by storing food in underground bulbs.

many of the flowering plants can grow, flower and produce their fruits and seeds at any time of year. Some tropical plants flower up to six times in one year, others only once every forty years or so.

4
Enemies and Survival

The emperor gum moth caterpillar feeds on gum tree leaves. Many plants are damaged by caterpillars.

Flowering Plants as Food for Animals

Flowering plants provide food for many animals. Insects feed on the nectar and pollen that the flowers produce, while birds, mammals and insects too, eat the fruit and seeds of many plants. Animals can cause damage when they eat the other parts of plants. Many flowering plants have their leaves and stems chewed by slugs, snails, beetles, grasshoppers and the caterpillars of butterflies and moths. Aphids and other plant bugs pierce into stems and suck out the sap, while underground, the roots may be attacked by slugs, beetles and the grubs of various flies. Larger animals such as rabbits, cows, goats, deer and horses eat plants too. Some of these **herbivores** graze on grass and other ground plants; others nibble at shrubs and trees.

Cows eat grass but avoid any poisonous plants that grow in the field.

or prickles. Many flowering plants contain poisons that can harm or even kill the animals that try to eat them. Some ooze out a poisonous sap as soon as they are touched or damaged; others have poisonous fruits or seeds. The stinging nettle is covered with tiny hairs that shoot out a stinging acid when an animal touches them.

Flowering plants have developed several ways of defending themselves from attack. Their stems are sometimes protected by a tough or waxy outer coat, which makes it difficult for insects to pierce through them; others are covered with thorns

Thistles are covered with sharp prickles that prevent most animals from eating them or trampling on them.

Surviving the Cold

Plants cannot grow at all if the weather becomes too cold. In countries where there is a cold winter, most perennials survive by resting until warmer weather returns. Woody plants have shoots that can survive above the ground. The parts of non-woody plants above ground often die away. However these plants stay alive below the ground, their supplies of

Many trees lose their leaves in winter. This helps save water and also means they do not waste energy in making food that is not needed.

stored food giving them the energy to grow when spring returns. Annuals survive by leaving seeds in the ground. Their hard outer coats protect them from frost during the winter.

In winter the soil is often frozen and plant roots cannot take in water.

It is therefore important that the plants lose as little moisture as possible. Evergreen plants, like holly and ivy, have thick, leathery leaves, which protects them from cold and keeps them from losing too much water.

Plants growing on the tops of mountains, or in the Arctic, live in cold, wintry weather for most of the year. They survive because they have **adapted** to these difficult conditions. Many of the plants grow close to the ground, forming small cushions or rosettes. Plants living in these cold, windswept places usually have difficulty in finding enough water. Their roots have to dig deep between cracks in the rocks, or spread out in the thin soil, to search for water when the soil thaws out in summer.

Like many mountain plants, the moss campion grows close to the ground, which helps it escape the cold wind.

Above *The Arctic lousewort is covered with soft, woolly hairs that help to trap warm air and moisture.*

Surviving in Hot, Dry Places

In deserts it may rain only once a year, or not at all. Many desert plants survive the long, dry spells by storing water inside their roots, stems or leaves. The agave plant stores water in its leaves. Cactus stems are often ridged or pleated so they can easily swell with water when it rains. Most desert trees and shrubs have small, spiny leaves. In a very bad drought, some plants shed their leaves completely.

Many desert plants have a thick, waxy outer skin, which prevents their losing water. Some have a covering of fine, woolly hairs, which protects them from drying winds. Most desert plants have shallow roots that spread widely through the thin soil, enabling them to soak up rain or dew. Desert trees usually have extremely long, deep roots, but they can only

Cacti are very well adapted to life in the desert. They store water in their fat, fleshy stems. Instead of leaves they have spines, which means they have less surface area from which to lose water.

survive where there is a deep underground supply of water.

Many desert plants survive the long, dry periods as seeds. When the rains come, they quickly burst into life, their flowers open, are pollinated and form seeds in just a few weeks, and then they die. Plants with a very short life cycle like this are called **ephemerals**.

A display of flowers after rain in the Kalahari Desert in southern Africa.

Water Plants

Some flowering plants live in wet places, such as ponds, lakes, rivers, bogs, swamps and marshes. Some of them live totally under water, some float on the surface with their roots dangling, while others live in waterlogged soil with only their roots

and the lower parts of their stems permanently under water.

Water holds much less oxygen than air, so water plants often find it difficult to get enough oxygen. To cope with this problem, many water plants have large air spaces inside their roots, stems and leaves. These air spaces connect inside the plant, which means that stored oxygen can easily pass to the parts needing it underwater. The air spaces may also act as floats, holding the leaves close to the surface where they can get enough light for photosynthesis.

Plants living in deeper water usually have weak, flimsy stems and thin, thread-like leaves that are supported by the water. Many underwater plants have small, weak

These mangrove trees have special prop roots that support them in the unstable mud of the swamps in which they grow.

The thin, flexible stems and leaves of the hornwort plant can bend and sway in the water without tearing or breaking.

Water lilies have large, flat, floating leaves and are well adapted to living in water.

roots. Unlike land plants, they do not rely entirely on their roots for their water supply – they are able to absorb water and other nutrients all over the surfaces of their stems and leaves.

It is not always easy for underwater plants to produce flowers and seeds, and many reproduce by forming new plants from buds or from parts of the parent plant that simply break.

5
Flowering Plants and Life on Earth

A selection of some of the fruits and vegetables we get from flowering plants.

Flowering Plants and People

People use flowering plants in hundreds of different ways. First and foremost, plants provide us, and our domestic animals, with food. Cereals are especially important – they are the fruits (called grains) of grasses, and include plants such as wheat, corn, barley, oats and rice. Cereals are rich in starch and provide the main food supply for most human populations.

Other important foods include peas, beans and lentils. These are all seeds of the pea family. We also eat underground roots and stems, such as carrots, turnips, potatoes and cassava, as well as a huge variety of other vegetables and fruits.

Many of our drinks, including fruit juices, wine, coffee, tea and cocoa, come from flowering plants. So do all our herbs and spices. Sugar is another plant product – it is extracted from

These grapes, growing in the Napa Valley in California, are ready to be picked and used to make into wine. Grapes can also be dried to make raisins.

sugar cane (a type of grass) in tropical countries, and from the sugar beet (a root) in other parts of the world.

People use flowering plants in many other ways too. The wood from trees provides us with fuel to burn, lumber for building and making furniture, and pulp for making paper. We use natural plant fibers, such as cotton, flax, jute and hemp, to weave into cloth or to make string, rope and matting. Many medicines and drugs are made from plants, while other useful substances include rubber, cork, oils, waxes and gums.

Conservation of Flowering Plants

Plants are a vital source of food for all animals on Earth. Animals cannot make their own food as plants do; they all depend on plants, even the meat-eaters, like lions, eagles or foxes. These **predators** eat other animals, such as deer or rabbits, which themselves survive by eating plants.

Dead plants are also important to life on Earth. Scavenging animals feed on them and their remains rot down to produce many valuable food substances, which are returned to the soil and used by other growing plants.

When plants make food by photosynthesis, they give off oxygen into the air. Most of the Earth's supply of oxygen comes from plants, and nearly every living creature needs oxygen to survive. So, without plants, life on Earth could barely exist.

Flowering plants are important in

As the world's population grows bigger, people cut down more and more trees for firewood, furniture or paper and to provide land for growing crops and grazing animals. This ruins the soil, destroys many valuable plants and upsets the balance of nature.

other ways too. They provide homes and shelter for many wild animals. They cover bare ground and their roots help to keep the soil in place.

Unfortunately, in many parts of the world, especially in tropical forests, large numbers of trees and other flowering plants are being destroyed by humans. If we want to survive in the future, we must protect our plants now. Otherwise the world will become a barren wilderness where nothing can live or grow.

An untouched area of tropical forest in Costa Rica.

6
How to Study Flowering Plants

Different flowering plants grow in different habitats. These are some of the plants you might find on the lower slopes of a mountain.

You can begin to study flowering plants by looking closely at the flowers in a garden or out in the country. Notice the various shapes, colors and designs of different flowers. Watch to see what insects come to visit them, or whether you think they are wind-pollinated.

Use a small magnifying glass to look closely at the plants; you should then be able to see tiny details, such as ridges and hairs on the surface of leaves and stems. Look closely into the flowers to see how the stamens and carpels are arranged, and whether you can see any nectaries.

Flowering plants are grouped into families, according to the structure of their stems, leaves, flowers and fruits. Try to decide which plants you think are closely related, and then find out by looking them up in a good reference book. You can begin to learn some plant names too.

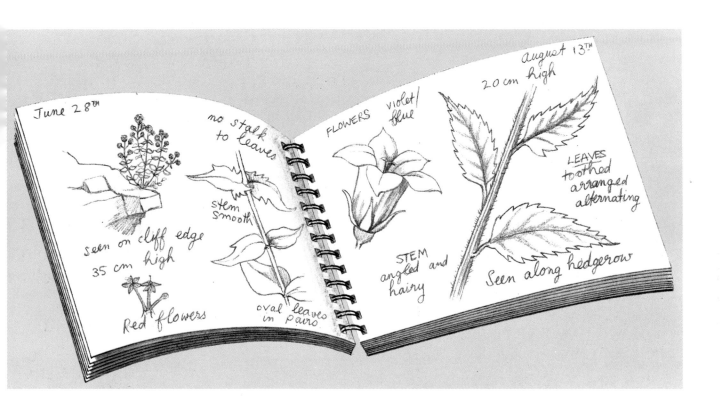

It is interesting to notice how different plants grow in different places. Try to study various habitats, such as a patch of boggy ground, an old wall, or a stretch of roadside verge. Make a list of the plants that grow there. You can study them at different

A good way to learn about anything in nature is to draw it. Keep a sketchbook to record your discoveries. Never pick wild flowers.

times of the year and then watch for any changes the following year.

Glossary

Adapted Suited for survival in a particular habitat.

Annuals Plants that grow, flower, produce seeds and die within one year.

Anther The upper part of a stamen containing the pollen.

Biennials Plants that take two years to complete their life cycle.

Bulb A swollen, underground, bud-like structure, composed of fleshy leaves in which food is stored.

Carpel One female unit of the flower, consisting of stigma, style and ovary.

Chlorophyll The green coloring in plants that enables them to carry out photosynthesis.

Corm A short, swollen underground stem (lasting only one year) in which food is stored.

Cotyledon The first leaf (or pair of leaves) of a plant, formed in the seed and often providing a food store during germination.

Embryo The young plant inside the seed.

Ephemerals Plants with a very short life cycle; some may produce several generations in one year.

Fertilize To join together the male and female sex cells of a flower so that a seed can grow from the fertilized ovule; also, to add nutrients to the soil.

Germinate To begin growth from the seed.

Habitat The place in which a plant or animal lives.

Herbivores Animals that eat mainly plants.

Minerals Chemicals found in soil or rocks.

Nectaries Special glands that produce nectar, found in many flowers. Nectar is a sweet, sugary liquid that attracts insects to flowers.

Ovary The part of the female flower containing the egg cells or ovules.

Ovules Female sex cells or eggs of a flower.

Perennials Plants that can live for several years, usually flowering each year.

Photosynthesis The process by which plants make food from simple chemicals, using the energy from sunlight.

Pollen Male sex cells of a flowering plant.

Pollination The transfer of pollen from the stamens to the stigma of a flower.

Predator An animal that kills and eats other animals.

Reproduction The process by which plants or animals produce others of their kind.

Rhizomes Horizontal underground stems, sometimes containing stored food, which last for more than one growing season.

Sepals The outer parts of a flower (usually green or brown), which protect the bud before it opens.

Stamens The male parts of a flower.

Stigma The part of a female flower (usually at the tip of the style) that receives pollen.

Stomata Openings, found mainly on the undersides of leaves, through which air and water vapor can pass. (Sing. stoma).

Style The stalk that connects the stigma with the ovary.

Veins Fine tubes within a leaf; they carry water and food and help support the leaf.

Finding Out More

The following books will help you find out more about flowering plants.

Beaudoin, Viola K. *Beaudoin Easy Method of Identifying Wildflowers: Over 475 Mountain Flowers.* Walnut Creek, CA: Evergreen Publishing, 1983.

Busch, Phillis S. *Wildflowers and the Stories Behind Their Names.* New York: Charles Scribner's Sons, 1977.

Fichter, George S. *Wildflowers of North America.* New York: Random House, 1982.

Forsthoefel, John and Gary Ransick. *Discovering Botany.* East Aurora, NY: DOK Publications, 1982.

Kipping, John. *North American Wildflowers.* San Francisco: Troubador Press, 1974.

Leutscher, Alfred. *Flowering Plants.* New York: Franklin Watts, 1984.

Podendorf, Illa. *Weeds and Wild Flowers.* Chicago, IL: Childrens Press, 1981.

Sabin, Louis. *Plants, Seeds and Flowers.* Mahwah, NJ: Troll Associates, 1985.

Simmons, John. *The Life of Plants.* Morristown, NJ: Silver Burdett, 1978.

Index

Picture Acknowledgments

All photographs from Oxford Scientific Films by the following photographers: T. Allen 38; G.I. Bernard *cover, frontispiece*, 8, 15, 17 (top), 18, 21, 24, 25 (top), 26, 28, 29, 31; J.A.L. Cooke 10, 30, 32; D. Clyne (Mantis Wildlife Films) 9; S. Dalton 23, 37 (right); M. Fogden 35, 37 (left); G.A. Maclean 13, 25 (bottom); S. Morris 22, 33 (top), 40, 42; K. Porter 20; A. Ramage 12; T. Shepherd 11, 14; Stouffer Enterprises, Inc. (Earth Scenes) 39; D. Thompson 17 (bottom), 27, 34, 36; P. & W. Ward 41; B.E. Watts 33 (bottom).